To
    Jim + Ann
We hope this book
brings you as much
Pleasure as your
Company did.
kind Regards
from   Graham + Ann
        May 1999

Leicestershire

Leicestershire

Michael Kilburn

Waterton Press Limited

First published in the United Kingdom in 1998 by
Frith Publishing an imprint of Waterton Press Limited.
Reprinted in 1999

British Library Cataloguing in Publication Data.

Michael Kilburn
Leicestershire

ISBN 1-84125-031-7

Reproductions of all the photographs in this book are
available as framed or mounted prints. For more
information please contact The Francis Frith Collection at
the address below quoting the title of this book and the
page number and photograph number or title.

The Francis Frith Collection,
'Friths Barn' Tefont, Salisbury, Wilts, SP3 5QP
E mail: bookprints@francisfrith.com
Web pages: www.francisfrith.com

Typeset in Bembo Semi Bold

Printed and bound in Great Britain by
WBC Limited, Bridgend, Glamorgan.

Contents

Francis Frith 1822-1898

Introduction
Francis Frith: A Victorian Pioneer

Francis Frith, the founder of the world famous photographic archive was a complex and multitudinous man. A devout Quaker and a highly successful and respected Victorian businessman he was also a flamboyant character.

By 1855 Frith had already established a wholesale grocery business in Liverpool and sold it for the astonishing sum of £200,000, equivalent of over £15,000,000 today. Now a multi-millionaire he was able to indulge in his irresistible desire to travel. As a child he had pored over books penned by early explorers, and his imagination had been stirred by family holidays to the sublime mountain regions of Wales and Scotland. "What a land of spirit-stirring and enriching scenes and places!" he had written. He was to return to these scenes of grandeur in later years to "recapture the thousands of vivid and tender memories", but with a very different purpose. Now in his thirties, and captivated by the new science of photography, Frith set out on a series of pioneering journeys to the Middle East, that occupied him from 1856 until 1860.

He took with him a specially-designed wicker carriage which acted as camera, dark-room and sleeping chamber. These far-flung journeys were full of intrigue and adventure. In his life story, written when he was sixty-three, Frith tells of being held captive by bandits, and fighting "an awful midnight battle to the very point of exhaustion and surrender with a deadly pack of hungry, wild dogs". He bargained for several weeks with a "mysterious priest" over a beautiful seven-volume illuminated Koran, which is now in the British Museum. Wearing full arab costume, Frith arrived at Akaba by camel seventy years before Lawrence of Arabia, where he encountered "desert princes and rival sheikhs, blazing with jewel-hilted swords".

During these extraordinary adventures he was assiduously exploring the desert regions of the Nile and recording the antiquities and people with his camera, Frith was the first photographer ever to travel beyond the sixth cataract. Africa, we must remember, was still the "Dark Continent", and Stanley and Livingstone's famous meeting was a decade into the future. The conditions for picture taking confound belief. He laboured for hours on end in his dark-room in the sweltering heat, while the volatile collodion chemicals fizzed dangerously in their trays. Often he was forced to work in tombs and caves where conditions were cooler.

Back in London he exhibited his photographs and was "rapturously cheered" by the Royal Society. His reputation as a photographer was made overnight. His photographs were issued in albums by James S. Virtue and William MacKenzie, and published simultaneously in London and New York. An eminent historian has likened their impact on the population of the time to that on our own generation of the first photographs taken on the surface of the moon.

Characteristically, Frith spotted the potential to create a new business as a specialist publisher of photographs. In 1860 he married Mary Ann Rosling and set out to photograph every city, town and village in Britain. For the next thirty years Frith travelled the country by train and by pony and trap, producing photographs that were keenly bought by the millions of Victorians who, because of the burgeoning rail network, were beginning to enjoy holidays and day trips to Britain's seaside resorts and beauty spots.

To meet the demand he gathered together a team of up to twelve photographers, and also published the work of independent artist-photographers of the reputation of Roger Fenton and Francis Bedford. Together with clerks and photographic printers he employed a substantial staff at his Reigate studios. To gain an understanding of the scale of Frith's business one only has to look at the catalogue issued by Frith & Co. in 1886. It runs to some 670 pages listing not only many thousands of views of the British Isles but also photographs of most major European countries, and China, Japan, the USA and Canada. By 1890 Frith had created the greatest specialist photographic publishing company in the world.

He died in 1898 at his villa in Cannes, his great project still growing. His sons, Eustace and Cyril, took over the task, and Frith & Co. continued in business for another seventy years, until by 1970 the archive contained over a third of a million pictures of 7,000 cities, towns and villages.

The photographic record he has left to us stands as a living monument to a remarkable and very special man.

Frith's dhow in Egypt *c*.1857

INTRODUCTION TO LEICESTERSHIRE

The photographs in this volume are historic documents. They record the interregnum between late Victorian development in Leicestershire and the post 1950's boom in housing and office building, which combined with accelerated building technology, to deliver the ubiquitous double-glazed window, and almost everything plastic. Notwithstanding the designation of Conservation areas by sensitive county authorities, which are, by definition, designed to protect the environment, attractive regular terraces and houses have become a hotchpotch of ill-matched windows and doors, through the weaknesses of conservation legislation in its basic form.

To many outsiders, Leicestershire is either to be slept through on the train into or out of St Pancras, or driven through at high speed on the M1 motorway. It is, in fact, an area worthy of   special notice, a multi-faceted county of heavy Triassic claylands in the east, and rocky granite and slate outcrops in the west. To insiders, The Shires are evocative words, conjuring up an image of rolling grasslands, sheep and nucleated villages evenly spaced across the Ordnance Survey map, often linked by straight hawthorn-lined Enclosure roads, green drove roads or more ancient ways, quickly proving the old adage that in the countryside you are rarely out of sight of a church spire. Under the grassland, history is preserved in the familiar "medieval" ridge and furrow patterns of selions and furlongs. Interestingly the patterns are generally referred to as medieval, but although recent archeological evidence points, in some places, to a pre-Conquest date, the remains as we see them must have been in use immediately before the late eighteenth or early nineteenth Enclosures. I came to this landscape as a child just after the war, when a Sunday outing meant picnicking amongst the hills and hollows of the deserted medieval village of Ingarsby, some four miles east of the city, but it was not until much later, as a schoolboy in 1950, that I came upon W.G. Hoskins wonderful little book - *The Heritage of Leicestershire*. Barrows and tumuli, deserted medieval villages, churches and monastic houses were all here, jumping out of the page, and it was through this chance find that a lifetime love affair with the county began.

Leicestershire is not a county of excesses, and the city will never have the same magnetic effect as York, Bath or Durham. Its one great house, Belvoir Castle, is strangely isolated amongst its lesser but equal neighbours such as Quenby, Baggrave, Withcote or Market Bosworth. Churches such as Stoke Golding, Kings Norton, Gadsby, Bottesford and Exton, with its tremendous series of monuments, have a beauty quite equal to those of the more lauded Midland counties of Northamptonshire or Warwickshire. The city with its extraordinary population explosion during the nineteenth century has a good collection of contemporary buildings. An enclave of eighteenth century houses survives mainly around St Martins Cathedral, but since the early 1960s little has taken place which could be called enhancement. The Inner Ring Road has swept through, in accordance with traffic engineers' cavalier schemes, leaving the historic Newarke Gateway ridiculously isolated and demolishing extensive areas of housing. The city centre has lost some of its visual allure with demolitions to accommodate the Shires shopping centre, but to step out of Trubshaw's Grand Midland Railway Station, to be greeted with the well-aired phrase - "Eh up me duck", is to be home.

ASFORDBY

The Leicestershire industrial landscape has never been dramatic, but the ironworks at Asfordby Hill provided a microcosmic taste of the North country. Built by the Holwell Iron Company in 1878 on the ironstone belt, the five blast furnaces brought with them an inevitable backwash. Once small and well sited above the River Wreake, the village absorbed an ultimately visually destructive share of the housing needed to cater for the inevitable influx of workers with their families, until the closure of the complex in 1958.

A211025   CHURCH LANE, ASFORDBY. Apart from All Saints, little of architectural quality has survived, except for a few rather handsome houses, the Rectory of 1808 and the Old Hall. This view of the church, and on to the river behind, retains a tranquil air uncommon to much of the village.

A211003   ALL SAINTS CHURCH, ASFORDBY The fifteenth century spire soars above the River Wreake on its south side, with the now rather mundane village Street to its north. Internally, little to detain the visitor, apart from the nave roofs with its stone heads and wooden angels.

A211008   THE OLD HALL, MAIN STREET, ASFORDBY. Formerly the manor house of about 1620, this find red brick building is now, itself, deteriorating. Sashed windows, within stone surrounds, under triple gables, grace a quietly elegant façade. Internally Jacobean woodwork survives as does a wooden spiral back stair. Facing Main Street is the early nineteenth century coach-house and stable to The Old Hall.

A211001   MAIN STREET, ASFORDBY. The late nineteenth century industrial face of the village percolates through the photograph, providing a dramatic contrast to Church Lane, which runs almost picturesquely away to the right of the cross.

A211020   THE RIVER WREAKE AT ASFORDBY. Out of the River Eye, to the east of Melton Mowbray, flows the River Wreake, slowly winding its way around the superb earthworks of Kirby Park and the former Augustinian priory at Kirby Bellars to the south of Asfordby village.

Ashby-de la-Zouch

A little further to the northwest and the market town of Ashby-de-la-Zouch would have been in Derbyshire. In the past this quiet town, which lies close to the remnants of the Leicestershire coalfields, was generally better known than it is today, finding an everlasting monument in the sweeping novels of Sir Walter Scott and in its spa which opened around 1822, with the erection of the rather beautiful, but now demolished, Ivanhoe Baths and the Royal Hotel.

A212029   THE CASTLE ASHBY-DE-LA-ZOUCH. Situated in the shadow of the grand church of St Helen's, the castle, now in the care of English Heritage, originated as a Norman manor house, to ultimately become the property, in the mid-twelfth century of the Breton La Zouch family. Probably the castle's most famous, or infamous owner was William Lord Hastings who was beheaded by King Richard III in 1483.

A212014   OLD COTTAGES, HILL STREET, ASHBY-DE-LA-ZOUCH. Pretty eighteenth century and earlier, brick and stone cottages which went to make up the Ashby referred to by Camden as "villa amoenissima", pre-dating the dramatic launch of the town as a health-restoring spa.

A212033   THE ROYAL HOTEL, STATION ROAD, ASHBY-DE-LA-ZOUCH. The Royal Hotel is an impressive brick and stone building, designed by the virtually unknown architect Robert Chaplin in 1826, employing a large porch of paired Greek Doric columns to impress those arriving in search of the invigorating spa waters, which were said to be good for rheumatism.

A212017   MARKET STREET, ASHBY-DE-LA-ZOUCH. A pleasant but rather undistinguished wide street, which was the scene of a Saturday market since it was granted in 1219. The photograph generally shows later Georgian flat fronted houses with shops thrust into their ground floors.

A212012   MARKET STREET, ASHBY-DE-LA-ZOUCH. The slightly overlarge Italianate Town Hall, along with the French Renaissance bank building of 1891, dominate an otherwise well ordered street scene. The buildings appear to be of later Georgian date, but the jetted timber framed house to the right speaks of hidden treasures to be found behind and within.

A212030   VIEW FROM ST HELEN'S CHURCH. ASHBY-DE-LA-ZOUCH. From St Helen's Church, west across the rooftops, to Our Lady of Lourdes R.C. Church and Holy Trinity Church in Kilwardby Street. In a well ordered townscape the countrywide low point of the early 1960's has clearly arrived at Ashby, with the larger building towards the bottom right of the photograph.

17

BARROW-UPON-SOAR

Situated about eight miles north of Leicester, the river and the limeworks are the village's main claims to any fame. Since at least the medieval period the lime produced at Barrow has, for building purposes, seen no better. Few buildings in the village are worthy of note, apart from the Old Men's Hospital founded by Humphrey Babington in 1686 and the Old Women's Hospital of 1825. One seventeenth century house of any note survives in Beveridge Street.

B514006   HOLY TRINITY CHURCH, BARROW-UPON-SOAR. Externally the Mountsorrel granite facing of the church gives it a hard, almost unwelcoming appearance. Most of the building work was carried out between 1863 and 1870, to the designs of Stevens and Robinson, a Derbyshire firm of architects. Internally there is a mid-seventeenth century monument of interest, to Theophilus Cave and one from the mid-eighteenth century to Martha Utber.

B514029   HIGH STREET, BARROW-UPON-SOAR. The rather barren appearance of the High Street exemplified in this photograph, regrettably sets the tenor of this large mainly red brick village. It is difficult not to greet, with a certain sadness, the intrusive "modern" post office to the right of the photograph.

B514032   THE BRIDGE AND RIVER, BARROW-UPON-SOAR. By 1086 the Soar Valley was well settled, and although the Domesday village of Barhou offers little to delight the visitor, the river has a watery magnetism which draws families from Leicester to its banks on warm summer days.

B5143271   THE BOATHOUSE, BARROW-UPON-SOAR. The charm of the river is highlighted in this classic composition of moored boats, overhanging trees, and a perfectly positioned swan – the ultimate vision of a lazy day spent away from traffic and stress.

BELVOIR CASTLE

Deriving from "beautiful view", the name equates with the French Belvedere, and is first recorded in 1130 as Belveder. By the mid-fifteenth century the original castle was ruinous, but it was rebuilt during the second quarter of the sixteenth century. Ruinous again by 1649, it was rebuilt at the wish of the Countess of Rutland by the pupil of Inigo Jones, Philip Webb. In 1801, the profilic, yet masterly architect, James Wyatt, was engaged to remodel the building. The task was in fact completed after fire partially destroyed the new work, by the Reverend Sir John Thoroton, Wyatt having died.

To the north of the castle in 1076, Robert de Todeni endowed a small Benedictine priory with only four monks, in which he and his wife could be buried. It was dissolved in 1538 and demolished. The bodies of the founder and his wife were recovered and reinterred in the present chapel.

Faced in yellow ironstone this fairytale composition is the ideal castle of nineteenth century romantic fiction, with its towers and crenellations breathing life into the Gothic fantasy world. The aerial photograph on the next page shows an apparently unstructured plan, but the castle is in fact, roughly rectangular around a central courtyard. On the righthand side of the building is the Regents Gallery, transformed by Wyatt from the earlier long gallery, and to the left is the Elizabeth Saloon, named after the fifth Duchess of Rutland. Outside the thick wooded cover, the more open land of the deer park is corrugated by medieval ridge and furrow of open field cultivation.

B633078   BELVOIR CASTLE FROM THE NORTH. Belvoir Castle is picturesquely situated some six miles to the west of Grantham, at the foot of a narrow spur of the country, jutting up between Nottinghamshire and Lincolnshire. Prominent for miles around, it was built menacingly by the Conqueror's standard bearer, Robert de Todeni, on an escarpment rising some two hundred feet above the surrounding countryside.

27861   BELVOIR CASTLE FROM THE NORTH-WEST. The classic view of the castle, contrasting the delicacy of the chapel, with its triple Gothic windows and pinnacled octagonal towers, with the somewhat more robust Windsor-like tower to its left.

BILLESDON

Billesdon is to be seen on foot. It is oblong in plan with the church at its southern end and the A47 to the north, running from east to west. Long abandoned medieval roads enter the village, in particular from the north, from Cold Newton, itself a shrunken medieval village, and from Galby to the south west, through the deserted medieval village of Frisby, into the narrow back lanes of Billesdon. Not picturesque in a picture book way, this is a village to absorb at leisure.

B593004   BILLESDON FROM THE EAST. This view, taken from the fields beyond the village, shows the broach spire of the church of St. John the Baptist, rebuilt in 1861, rising above the very attractive slate and stone roofscape to a village of mainly brick and ironstone faced houses.

B593001 BILLESDON FROM THE SOUTH WEST. Close to the village, medieval ridge and furrow cultivation has been preserved in its meadows and closes, and on its western edge it is the back lanes which seem to be in an unusually complete state. Many houses have their front doors opening directly onto alleyways and paths, all apparently higgledy-piggledy, saying much about the layout and texture of medieval village life, always under the shadow of the church.

B593006 BACK STREET, BILLESDON. Diverse materials make up the warp and weft of this village. At the southern end of Back Street, mud walls survive opposite the seventeenth century Old School building, and the turn-of-the century Stone House displays the builder's artful use of a cheaper brick shell adorned with a more expensive stone front.

B593002   THE MARKET PLACE, BILLESDON. The photograph shows, in the main, modest cottages of seventeenth and eighteenth century date, more impressive houses are to be found behind the camera. Until recently the long established Geary Brothers, builders and joiners, occupied the building to the right of the shot. The Friday market was discontinued at the end of the eighteenth century, Not only does the ancient "Jurassic Trackway" run on a north-south line to the east of the village towards Tilton-on-the Hill, but a Neolithic road from Leicester, eastwards towards Ingarsby, skirts the northern boundary of the parish. In its turn that same road line was utilised to demarcate part of the boundary to the Saxon estate belonging to Tochi, now translated as Tugby, a village three miles to the east of Billesdon.

In this north western sector of a remarkable parish it is possible to go back two thousand years at a glance, from the ancient trackway to an abandoned railway line, courtesy of Dr. Beeching. Also within this very small area is Billesdon Coplow, a prominent wooded hill, and within its lee Botany Bay fox covert, which is thus clearly dated too soon after 1788, when the infamous penal colony was established in Australia.

BOTTLESFORD

The most northerly village in Leicestershire, this large parish sits comfortably on the River Devon. An expansive village, its buildings of interest tend to be distributed rather than grouped. The Rectory in Church Street is not without interest, while Flemings Almshouses and the Earl of Rutland's Hospital should be noted. Flemings Bridge of the seventeenth century lies close by St Mary's Church.

B515003   ST MARY'S CHURCH, BOTTESFORD. The recessed crocketted spire of St Mary's dominates the countryside around. Inside, the church houses one of the finest collections of monuments in the country. Superb works of art commissioned since 1543 to mark the resting places of the Earls of Rutland, include two of considerable elegance by Grinling Gibbons.

CASTLE DONINGTON

The village, with its market place and church, grew up around the castle in much the same way as Totnes in Devon or Warkworth in Northumberland. The grid pattern of streets providing a vital clue to its medieval origins.

Of the castle buildings nothing survives, in fact the site is now given over to houses and gardens. The castle being eventually forsaken for the more amenable pleasure of the hall and park, but it was not until the parish enclosure of 1777 that tightly packed farmers moved out into more airy accommodation in the surrounding fields, many of which are now obliterated by the noisy East Midlands Airport.

C430014   The Church of St Edward King and Martyr, Castle Donington. Seen here from the south, the parish church with its unusual dedication is an amalgam of parts up to the fifteenth century, when the porch was added on the south side. Apart from the east window by Kemp and Co. and a few minor monuments, there is little here of detail to interest the visitor.

C430003   THE KEY HOUSE, HIGH STREET, CASTLE DONINGTON. Dating from the turn of the seventeenth century, the Key House is probably the best of Castle Donington's vernacular buildings. Timber framed, it has a two-storey porch decorated with lozenges, a most unusual feature for its date.

C430005   MARKET STREET, CASTLE DONINGTON. The photograph is dominated by a brick and stone building typical of its turn-of-the-century date, but in this southern sector of the town earlier houses are to be found, including a stone-faced building in Apiary Gate of around 1670.

C430007   Cottages at Kings Mills, Castle Donington. This terrace of almost picturesque millworker's cottages now sits quietly, adjacent to the isolated and decaying great water wheels which once powered the mills. Originally for corn milling, the mills in their later life were given over to a variety of industrial uses.

C430009   Kings Mills, Castle Donington. Some two miles to the west of Castle Donington, the attractive and once powerful watermills are situated close to Donington Hall, itself a good late eighteenth century house designed by the prolific architect, William Wilkins, whose other works include the National Gallery and University College, London. A fire in 1927 took much of the complex but the extant group is attractive and a detour repays the effort expended. The building in the foreground of the photograph was Gothicized in the early nineteenth century.

C430008   THE RIVER TRENT AT KINGS MILLS, CASTLE DONINGTON. A leisurely view typical of many to be seen on the rivers Trent and Soar, but the need to protect the crossing of this river provided the initial *raison d'etre* for the castle and the village.

C430004   BONDGATE, CASTLE DONINGTON. Although quiet, even in 1955, Bondgate is on the line of the turnpike road between Long Easton and Ashby-de-la-Zouch. We can still appreciate in these photographs the quality of houses and shops, before the destructive work of the modern window salesman spread like a rash over the country.

C430001   HIGH STREET, CASTLE DONINGTON. Bondgate crosses Mount Pleasant to become the restrained High Street on the south side of the village rising up to Hill Top. The photographer looks back down the hill past nineteenth century houses towards the village centre.

COALVILLE

It is not possible to think of Coalville, without thinking of Desford, Whitwick, Ellistown and Merry Lees, all pits in the Leicestershire coalfields which provided generations of miners with a dangerous, unforgiving living, until the end arrived with the closure of Bagworth Colliery in 1991.

For some five hundred years the area has been mined, but in 1824 deep mining arrived at Whitwick, and by 1833 Longlane had been renamed. The town grew with the expansion of the industry to blend inexorably with the surrounding unloveliness of the pit-heads and tips, and the railway which opened in 1833. Much of the evidence of coal mining has now disappeared, but at Snibstone, to the north-west of the town, a sanitized glimpse of mining life can be had at the Discovery Park.

C4323126   BELVOIR ROAD, COALVILLE. The photograph shows perhaps one of the less depressing views that can be taken in the town, but even in 1956, the pattern of things to come is readily apparent in the intrusive shopfront and canopy pushed into a reasonably attractive façade.

C432053   LEICESTER ROAD, COALVILLE. A depressing series of small-scale shops line the main road, which is soon to sweep in more peaceful mode under Bardon Hill. Few of the shop fronts are of any quality and in particular "Telefusion" serves to herald the dawn of the visually unattractive 1960's.

C432045   JACKSON STREET, COALVILLE. Small, well-mannered cottages set this later nineteenth century pre-mass street parking scene. The bay windowed house to the left of the photograph remains intact but neglected, while shops have taken over the remainder.

C432007 THE CLOCK TOWER, COALVILLE. Almost out of shot on the right-hand side of the photograph is probably the best quality structure in the town. Designed by Henry Collings in 1926 and faced in brick and stone, the Clock Tower overshadows Memorial Square and the market place.

C432054 SHOPPING CENTRE, COALVILLE. Any town, anywhere, the epitomy of the Borough Architects' brave new world of the early 1960s. More shopper friendly, enclosed arcades have taken the place of the violently unattractive centres, and no-one can mourn their passing.

Mount St Bernard Abbey

Situated on the edge of the Charnwood Forest, some two miles from Whitwick, Mount St Bernard Abbey, which was founded here in 1835, was the first Cistercian house in England since the dissolution of the monasteries. The buildings occupy land given to the monastery in 1835 by Ambrose Lisle March - Phillips of Grace Dieu Manor and sponsored by the Earl of Shrewsbury. Much of the building work was done by the community.

C432035   MOUNT ST BERNARD ABBEY FROM THE NORTH-WEST. This monastic group faced in local granite rubble with ashlar dressings was carefully designed by A.W.N. Pugin, to meet the relatively austere needs of a Cistercian house. Completed in 1841, the Guest House with its central carriage opening occupies much of the photograph. To the left of the shot are the lancet lights to the Monastic Choir, of 1843-4.

C432034   MOUNT ST BERNARD ABBEY FROM THE EAST. The church to the left of the photograph remained incomplete until just prior to the outset of World War II, construction work having stopped in 1844 through a lack of finances. The well-proportioned tower, which sits above the sanctuary, was designed by Leicester architect, Albert Herbert and completed in 1939.

C4323001   THE CLOCK TOWER, MOUNT ST BERNARD ABBEY. The clock tower with its slated spire-like roof sits on the western range of the claustral buildings, above the enclosed garden to its west and the small cloister to its east. The tower was added in 1871.

C4323004   THE CALVARY, MOUNT ST BERNARD ABBEY. This dramatic view of the Calvary, which lies to the north of the Abbey buildings was taken shortly after its completion, with the addition of the figure of Christ in 1965, although it was begun in 1847.

COSBY

Cosby is not enhanced by the presence of the M1 motorway on its eastern flank, or by the fact that the horny hand of industrial south Leicester has touched the village. Of its early history little remains, except a few houses and the Church of St Michael with its fifteenth century tower and some earlier fabric. Quite rare for Leicestershire, a cruck-framed barn survives in part at Church Farm close to the church.

During the sixteenth century, the village was dominated by the Bent family, firstly William and subsequently his son Thomas, bought land here on a large scale, until by 1550 he owned well over 600 acres within the parish. By contrast, the vicar of Cosby was, in 1615, complaining bitterly that he could not support his family on a wage of under five pounds a year.

C433008   MAIN STREET, COSBY. The openness of the village is readily apparent in this photograph, as it ranges along a brook, criss-crossed by modest Urban District Council railed footbridges. Regrettably, the main nineteenth century two-storey buildings fail to enhance the scene to a degree that can be called picturesque.

C433007   THE BROOK, COSBY. The brook here somehow appears to be little cared for, with its chipped concrete posts arrayed along weedy banks. To the right of the photograph is a row of uninteresting nineteenth/twentieth century houses, and to the left, and of an earlier era, the three-storey, three-bay brick farmhouse, so common in Leicestershire villages. The overall scene is not enhanced by telephone wires and a rather nasty bus shelter.

C434011   COTTESMORE, RUTLAND. Originally a Saxon estate or soke, Rutland provides a visual feast of limestone and ironstone villages; a rolling, spired landscape of hedges and walls which the hunt can, in the main, take in its stride. A tiny county which it seems, apart from blips such as the cement works at Ketton, has never, on the surface, moved into any industrial age, or even less, into an age of mass communication.

Great Bowden

The Lordship of Great Bowden, a royal soke, and Market Harborough has always been as one, although a Domesday population of 49 was recorded at Great Bowden; the origins of Market Harborough are of the later twelfth century when it grew out of the village fields. In 1776, enclosures transformed the parish from four great medieval common fields to a pattern of straight fences and quick-grow planting, a process unwelcome to many and translated by Northamptonshire poet John Clare, into his *cris de coeur,* "Enclosure" where he says:

Enclosure came, and trampled on the grave
Of labourers rights, and left the poor a slave:
And memories pride, ere want to wealth did bow.
In both the shadow and the substance now.

The Grand Union Canal was driven into the west of the village early in the nineteenth century, and some fifty years later the railway arrived to herald an industrial age.

72275   THE GREEN AND VILLAGE, GREAT BOWDEN. This photograph, taken in 1922, shows this Domesday village, now much consumed by the tentacles of Market Harborough's suburbs, with its large irregular green and attractive houses, some dating back to 1567 and 1664, and Stone House in main Street to 1671. The stumpy spire of the mainly fifteenth century church of St Peter and St Paul pokes above the rooftops, readily identifiable by its high lucarnes.

Of ancient Hinchelie nothing remains. Of twelfth century Hinkelai the flattened castle mound has little to say, and the small Benedictine cell founded here around 1175 was disbanded prior to the Reformation. Of the parish church of The Assumption of St Mary, the fourteenth century tower oversees much that is Victorian, with some work in 1877 by that rather uninspiring of architects, Ewan Christian.

It was in 1640 that the seeds of a successful industrial future were sown at Hinckley, with the arrival of the home stocking frame industry. Houses were rapidly adapted to accommodate the new machines, and prosperity reigned until setbacks in the early 1800's caused a total reversal of fortunes for the townsfolk. Although dominated by Leicester's hosiery industry, later nineteenth century textile and boot and shoe factories were built in the town bringing, in their wake, streets of red brick workers houses. Not really a place to saunter round for pleasure on a summer's evening.

H266010　　CASTLE STREET, HINCKLEY. A collection of almost classic cars parked on both sides of the street, issues a warning of things to come in the small towns around Leicestershire. In a street of mainly late-nineteenth and early twentieth century buildings, the uncomfortable all-purpose shop fronts of the 1960s on the left of shot, warns of an equal disaster in the world of architecture. Note the original shop fronts in the building to the right of the photograph.

H26006 Castle Street, Hinckley. Ladies in hats, and skirts below the knee point unmistakably to a date in the mid-1960s, reinforced by the presence of a "Silver Cross" pram. A few late Georgian buildings brighten up this otherwise dull street-scene. At least the shops still retain well-mannered fronts.

IBSTOCK

The Stoc of Ibba, a usage often allied to a monastic place, but here to a personal name. The settlement grew up in the Leicestershire coalfields along with its close neighbours, Coalville, Nailstone, Bagworth and Ellistown. The discovery of suitable clay for brick making in 1830 led to the opening of a second industry, which continues today. Not a tourist Mecca.

148003　　ST DENY'S CHURCH, IBSTOCK. Archbishop Laud was at sometime rector of this rather fine church, which groups close to the eighteenth century vicarage at the southern end of this mining town. Unusually, almost entirely of the fourteenth century, it has few interior features to detain the visitor.

KEGWORTH

Now a rather benighted industrial village on the River Soar, Kegworth's origins lay in its medieval weekly market and annual fairs. The arrival of framework knitters heralded its transformation, culminating in a dour expansion in redbrick housing and hosiery factories. Old houses of some merit are to be found in London Road, around the High Street and Packington Hill. The grand church of St Andrew, although internally quite dull justifies a visit.

K130008   THE LOCK, KEGWORTH. To the east of the village, a timeless view of an industry wiped out by the growth of the national railway system. Once utilised to deliver raw materials and take away the finished products to Derby or to Leicester, the waterway is basically reduced to the status of a leisure facility.

K139034   VIEW FROM ST ANDREWS CHURCH, KEGWORTH. A view which highlights the growth of industrial Kegworth. In 1965 uncomfortably large utilitarian factory/stores nestle close to the church, among the irregular tiled roofs of an earlier era.

KIBWORTH BEAUCHAMP

The parish of Kibworth, originally bracketed together Kibworth Beachamp, Kibworth Harcourt and Smeeton Westerby, sharing the mother church of St Wilfred, which stands prominently on the north-south link road between the two Kibworths. Beauchamp was added to the original name through *Walter de Beauchamp*, Lord of the Manor around 1130. A red brick village, there are a few buildings of interest, such as the seventeenth century Stuart House in Station Street and the Old Manor House in the High Street. Following the enclosure of the village around 1797, many agricultural workers were forced to find a new living in the hosiery industry.

K119019   THE SQUARE FROM THE WEST, KIBWORTH BEAUCHAMP. George Lynn advertises his wares with considerable vigour on the south side of the "triangular" square, originally called Cross Bank. Nothing appears in the photograph to shake the post-war calm of the village, bypassed on its eastern side by the busy A6. The telephone box serves as a vivid reminder of so many destroyed, and replaced by ill-conceived 1990's substitutes.

K119002   THE CRICKET GROUND, KIBWORTH
BEAUCHAMP. The cricket field, a focal point
of village life, where summer upon summer
old rivalries are played out. Where winter
game plans, hatched in the local pub can
produce unlikely heroes or fall apart in
minutes. The battlefield - its all here, in a
small probably balding grass square.

K119033   THE OLD MILL, KIBWORTH
HARCOURT. Dated 1711, this last post-mill in
the county, ceased working in 1912. With its
two pairs of stones the design is such that the
weaterboarded superstructure revolves round a
central post, ensuring that the four great sails
are always in the optimum position to take
advantage of any available wind.

KIRBY MUXLOE

Although originally a village in its own right, Kirby Muxloe had the misfortune to be situated both close into Leicester on its western fringe and, at the same time, close to the Leicestershire coalfields. Sadly it is a boring patch of semi-detached Leicester and industrial Braunstone. Devotees of the great Victorian architect, William Butterfield, will find some interest in his village school of 1857.

K126002   ST BARTHOLOMEWS CHURCH, KIRBY MUXLOE. A pleasant enough small church on the Desford road, originally of the fourteenth century, it is to some extent enhanced by the later tower on its south side. Internally the building does not justify a search for the key should it be locked.

K126004   KIRBY MUXLOE CASTLE. In fact a fortified manor house, the beauty of the castle resides to a great extent in the wonderful colour of its brickwork. Built by Lord Hastings of Ashby-de-la-Zouch, the building is cared for by English Heritage in its usual exemplary manner. The moated house dates from 1480 and although lacking the photogenic qualities of a Bodiam Castle, it is rewarding to the visitor.

LEICESTER

Roman Leicester occupied some hundred acres to the west of the Clock Tower, developing around the Forum on a standard pattern of gridded streets. After about AD 400 the area became part of the Kingdom of Mercia, and subsequently a part of the Danelaw, identified in the 'by' and 'ton' endings to many surrounding village names. Leicester Castle was built soon after the Norman Conquest, and by the fourteenth century the present open market was established, along with markets for grain, cattle, sheep and fish, among others. Comparatively little survives of the seventeenth and eighteenth century fabric of the town, but during the nineteenth century explosion in the hosiery and boot and shoe industries, the population grew fourteen-fold to over 200,000. This expansion continued into the twentieth century absorbing a number of villages such as Aylestone, Braunstone and Humberstone, in semi-detached 1930s ribbon development. A Garden City experiment at Humberstone, conceived with Bedford Park and Hampstead Garden Suburb in west and north London in mind, came to little, with only 95 houses built by 1915. At the turn of the twentyfirst century housing estates of little virtue, i.e. Hamilton, continue to eat away fields and hedgerows until the next outer layer of villages is swallowed.

L144069   THE ROMAN FORUM AND JEWRY WALL, LEICESTER. The remains of Ratae Corieltauvi, the origins of the city and a regional capital, lie adjacent to the superb Saxon church of St Nicholas, seen here in the centre of the photograph. The forum and basilica were excavated by Kathleen Kenyon. The remains are situated at the top of the High Street and are a must, particularly for the first-time visitor to the City.

L144091   PRINCE RUPERT'S GATEWAY, CASTLE YARD, LEICESTER. The mid-twelfth century Great Hall of Robert le Bossu survives in Castle Yard and has, up to modern times, been in use as an Assizes Court and Crown Court. In 1645 the castle was besieged by Prince Rupert and King Charles, and captured only to be retaken by Parliamentarians following the Royalist defeat at Naseby. The gateway has been ruined since 1832. Masked by the gate is the collegiate church of St Mary de Castro, with an external beauty, but a dull interior.

L144025   THE GUILDHALL, GUILDHALL LANE, LEICESTER. Leicester grew rapidly in the eighteenth and nineteenth centuries, but it continued to be governed from its small medieval Guidhall until 1876. Situated among the somewhat reduced remains of the buildings of Georgian Leicester, now tightly grouped in New Street, Peacock Lane and Friar Lane, the Guildhall is overshadowed by St Martins Cathedral (upgraded in 1927 from parish church status). The spire of the church is of some moment, but worked on internally by G.E. Street and J.L. Pearson at the end of last century. It has a rather lack-lustre feel, which is unfortunate. To the rear of the Guildhall, in 1949, was Alderman Newton's Boys Grammar School, the resited eighteenth century foundation of Alderman Gabriel Newton, who now lies buried in the churchyard of All Saints, High Cross Street. A visit to the Guildhall with its amazing fourteenth century timbered Great Hall of the Corpus Christi Guild and intimate inner courtyard of All Saints, High Cross Street is worthwhile.

L144093   THE TUDOR GATEHOUSE, THE CASTLE, LEICESTER. Dating from the mid-fifteenth century, this attractive timbered house makes a fine entrance to Castle Yard from Castle Street. To the left, but out of shot, the Church of St Mary de Castro completes a remarkable fine group.

L144074 THE TOWN HALL, HORSEFAIR STREET, LEICESTER. Thirty years prior to the building of the new Town Hall, Leicester was in a dreadful sanitary condition, with privies literally over-flowing into the streets, and it was not until the mid 1850s that piped water came to the town, along with the first sewers. By the 1870s facilities were expanding, and with this expansion came a new bureaucracy.

L144118 DE MONTFORT HALL, UNIVERSITY ROAD, LEICESTER. A surprisingly spry 85-year-old building, the De Montfort Hall shows little sign of ageing. Designed by architect Shirley Harrison, the building is well-sited close to Victoria Park, and to Lutyen's War Memorial, dedicated to those who fell in the First World War. To the rear of the Hall is the university campus with buildings by Denys Lasdun and James Stirling.

L144125   INTERIOR OF DE MONTFORT HALL, LEICESTER. With clear visibility and excellent acoustics, De Montfort Hall is one of the Midland's finest concert venues. Over the years it has heard every kind of music, and played host to many school speech days.

L144002   EASTGATE, LEICESTER. To the young in Leicester in 1949, the Clock Tower seemed like the centre of the universe, and life revolved around it guided by policemen on point duty. Holidays were generally taken at Skegness, Mablethorpe or Great Yarmouth, and pre-television entertainment was fairly extravagant with seven cinemas in the town centre, including the Floral Hall, along with three live theatres. Within two miles of the Clock Tower, local cinemas abounded, only to be swept away in the 1960s purge, including the rather magnificent Trocadero at Humberstone, replaced by a petrol station.

L144012   THE CLOCK TOWER, LEICESTER. The Gothic Clock Tower, designed by local architect Joseph Goddard in 1868 is decorated with pinnacles and canopies, along with four Leicester worthies including Alderman Gabriel Newton and Simon de Montfort. Beyond Corts Limited, can be seen the dominant dome of the Opera House, demolished in 1960, where each year the Christmas pantomine was staged, and appreciated with thunderous applause.

L144013   BELGRAVE GATE, LEICESTER. In a road of rather mundane buildings is the Palace Theatre, a remarkable building designed in a Moorish style by the Robert Adam of theatre design, Frank Matcham, for Moss Empires in 1901, with a seating capacity of 2,750. After some difficult years the theatre was demolished in 1959. The fine spire of St Marks Church of 1870, makes a worth while visual stop to this view north.

L144016   MARKET STREET, LEICESTER. The Edwardian and Victorian buildings in this part of the City are efficient without being distinctive. Closing the view south is the former General Accident Building, 1930, which Pevsner rather unkindly sums up as "a vile, impertinent lump".

L144017   BELVOIR STREET, LEICESTER. Centre of photograph is the dome of the Grand Hotel built in 1898 to the designs of Cecil Ogden, and dismissed by Pevsner as "of no architectural value", perhaps an over critical view. In Belvoir Street in 1949, Cowlings Record Shop was much frequented by Leicester's youth, who could sit in booths and hear the records before deciding whether or not to buy.

L144032   GRANBY STREET, LEICESTER. Banks abound in Granby Street, The Italianate National Westminster of 1869, The Midland, a Gothic creation with its French pavilion roof, and the Yorkshire Penny Bank opposite the Grand Hotel, being probably the most striking of all. Also in Granby Street is the sparkling turn-of-the-century Turkish Café offering a breath of the orient.

L144104   GALLOWTREE GATE, LEICESTER. The commemorative front, placed in 1894, of the former Thomas Cook building overlooking the Clock Tower, is, indeed special. The building on the left of shot fronts the open market, said to be the biggest, at least in Europe, with access ways running between the shops.

L144035   GRANBY STREET, LEICESTER. As Granby Street sweeps right towards the Clock Tower, the photograph clearly illustrates the unspectacular variety of buildings to be seen in the city centre. At the time of this photograph there are no roof extensions, few ugly street signs and no pedestrianisation.

L144007   HUMBERSTONE GATE, LEICESTER. Looking back, how well ordered this street scene appears, with virtually no cars, only rumbling trams, and great six-wheeler buses. The Bell Hotel speaks of genteel days, and Lewis's store on the right speaks of a more pressurised era of merchandising in the 1930's. Sadly a high proportion of the buildings in this photograph have, in recent years, been demolished.

LOUGHBOROUGH

The medieval street pattern, the parish church of All Saints and a ruined thirteenth century Hall House, which emerged in 1962 during the demolition of the rectory, serves as the very scant evidence of old Loughborough.

Second in size to the City itself, this rather dull, red brick town was established, with an open market by 1221 and with the November Fair following seven years later. Eleven miles from Leicester, and on the Leicester/Derby road, turnpiked in 1726, the towns coaching trade was assured. In 1794 the River Soar was canalised, and with this new accessibility to the waterway network, the hosiery and engineering industries began to settle locally. To ensure the towns long term future in commerce, the railway arrived in 1840, not only to transport the town's products, but also to carry coal from nearby pits. In more recent years the town has bathed in the glory of its university.

L197050   MARKET PLACE, 1955, LOUGHBOROUGH. A model medieval market place in its wide, long configuration. There is little remarkable about the buildings, which are mainly of the nineteenth century. All Saints Church, seen in the background, grew in tandem with the town's increasing prosperity and justifies a close inspection.

L197009   MARKET PLACE, 1955, LOUGHBOROUGH. Lloyds's bank, on the left of the photograph provides a datum from which the quality of Loughborough's architecture can be measured. Apart from a few earlier buildings in the shot, all is rather mediocre. Restrained signs and shop fronts and no unsightly yellow lines, speak of an almost forgotten era.

L197003   HIGH STREET, 1955, LOUGHBOROUGH. A policeman on point duty sets the tone of this well-regulated scene. Above Harris's shop is a glimpse of industrially prosperous Loughbrough, with Brush Electrical and J.Taylors' Bell Foundry in Freehold Street, being among the more widely know resident companies.

L197101   MARKET PLACE, 1965, LOUGHBOROUGH. Since 1955 two architectural nonentities have appeared on the right of the photograph to mar the already indifferent quality of the market place, and road markings are becoming a prominent feature. The Italianate Town Hall dominates the street scene with its rather old bell-cote.

L197008   HIGH STREET, 1955, LOUGHBOROUGH. The High Street (A6 Leicester/Derby road), becomes Leicester Road as it runs south. A few earlier buildings survive on the left-hand side of the photograph, but the right is dominated by uninspired, even dreary, red brick Edwardian buildings.

L197021   DEVONSHIRE SQUARE, LOUGHBOROUGH. Although the Gothic hotel has some claim to architectural quality it is the Art Deco intruder which catches the eye. Faced in cream tiles and built in 1936, the cinema must have proved irresistible to its original audiences seeking escape into fantasy, as did their predecessors in the elaborate world of Victorian theatre.

L197001   CHURCH GATE, LOUGHBOROUGH. A bracketed gas lamp, original timber shop fronts and sashed windows, along with a lovely advertisement for Halford's Cycle Accessories creates an unusually attractive street scene. Such a complete ensemble would be difficult to find today.

L197026 COLLEGE GATE, ASHBY ROAD, LOUGHBOROUGH. Hazlerigg Hall and Rutland Hall, built to the designs of the then County Education Committee Architect in 1939, in a neo-Tudor style were the original halls of residence to Loughborough College. Expanded after 1952 the now Loughborough University occupies a campus approaching 250 acres.

L197045 QUEENS PARK, GRANBY STREET, LOUGHBOROUGH. The view from the typically landscaped municipal park is enlivened by the attractive Central Library building of 1903, with its Baroque façade and conical roof crowned by a timber belt turret. At the side of the library are examples of the town's modest turn-of-the-century housing stock.

The Carillon, Queens Park, Loughborough. This 151 ft high, 47 bell brick carillon was designed by Sir Walter Tapper, and erected in 1923 as the towns tribute to the fallen of the First World War. The bells were cast by Taylors, whose foundry was established in Loughborough in 1839 and with Whitechapel, London, comprises England's only surviving bell founders.

L197017

Lutterworth

Little more than a village before the eighteenth century, the town is famous for its association with John Wycliff, a religious reformer and translator of the bible, who was condemned by the Pope in 1377 for his outspoken attacks on clerical wealth and privilege. Wycliffe came to Lutterworth in the wake of this condemnation as rector, under the protection of John of Gaunt, where he was to die in 1384. He did not rest in peace, his remains being exhumed and burnt in 1428 and the remnants thrown into the River Swift. The church, which is not without interest,has a good white marble monument to Wycliffe in the south aisle, by Richard Westmacott of 1837.

The town, with its town hall designed in 1836 by Joseph Alcysius Hansom, inventor of the Hansom cab, comprises buildings mainly of the earlier nineteenth century, but notwithstanding this, the High Street, Market Place and Market Street are worthy of inspection. In 1218 the Hospital of St John The Baptist was established at Lutterworth for the poor and aged, but it was dissolved and lost about 1580.

L307005   CHURCH STREET, LUTTERWORTH. Church Street has about it an almost faded Dickensian air, in tune with a town whose better days appear to be past, which is a great pity. The photograph shows congenial, modest, mostly early nineteenth century buildings, with a series of shop fronts pre-dating the ugliness of late twentieth century aluminium framing and internally illuminated fascia signs.

L307001   THE DENBIGH ARMS, HIGH STREET, LUTTERWORTH. A typical atmospheric Georgian hotel on the steep hill up through the town. Although the front of the building is of early nineteenth century appearance, earlier brickwork and, indeed, some signs of timber framing within the buildings, speak of a longer history.

MARKET BOSWORTH

The Dixies brought a certain amount of prosperity to the town when they built the hall at the end of the seventeenth century in the shadow of the church, which at the end of the previous century was itself providing a particularly rich living. From the red brick house it is a rewarding saunter through the park to Sutton Cheney church, and to the Battlefield Centre at Ambion Hill Farm. The battle, fought on the 22 August 1485, is easily visualised through illustrative boards set discreetly round the site. An easy walk back to the town completes a circle of about five miles, but tea and cakes are not easily come by to round off the walk.

Fortunately the town totally escaped the destructive influences that assailed its close neighbours in the coalfields, such as Desford and Nailstone. Fox coverts spread around the town are a reminder that Leicestershire provides ideal hunting country, but for the lovers of speed the motor race track at Kirkby Mallory provides more than adequate entertainment.

M233001   The Town, Market Bosworth. Since the thirteenth century there has been a market here, and the buildings in the town centre reflect a gentle change rather than a dramatic fluctuation of fortune at any one time. Single storey dormered cottages sit comfortably, with the later elegance of the flat-fronted Georgian house further along the street.

M233015 THE MARKET SQUARE, MARKET BOSWORTH. Market Bosworth was granted the privilege of a Wednesday market in 1285, and the small town was one of 29 in the country to combine this with an annual fair. In a primarily subsistence orientated world, the market of the thirteenth century proved an efficient way for producers to sell their surplus products. More often than not the privilege of establishing a market had to be bought, and the lord needed to be sure of a return on his investment.

The Market Square, which here takes a triangular form, is surrounded by modest, attractive, mainly eighteenth century houses, apart from the Grammar School, which, to some extent, raises the scale. The presence of a traditional, but modern cross completes the picture. Today the square has regrettably taken on a more regimented appearance, with a regularised car park behind concrete bollards, but it is, in its essentials, little changed. Situated away from major routeways the town has derived its fame from the Battle of 1485, when Henry Tudor, later Henry VII defeated Richard III on Ambion Hill to its south.

M233025 ST PETERS CHURCH, MARKET BOSWORTH. Grouping with the late seventeenth century Hall, the building exhibits all the qualities of a fully fledged town church, with its fine tower and recessed spire. The dearth of old headstones does not enhance its setting, which deserves much better. Inside the church, is a monument of note to the Rev. John Dixie, 1719, incorporating a wonderfully sad fluid sculpture of a mourning woman.

MARKET HARBOROUGH

The town developed as a deliberately created market centre at the crossing of the River Welland, growing up within the parish of Great Bowden, some time around 1175, being granted a weekly market in 1202. The superb church with its spire, said to be among the best in England, has no churchyard and no rights to carry out burials, this responsibility being incumbent upon the mother church. In the eighteenth century Market Harborough was little more than one great market street, but with the turnpiked road and the arrival of the Grand Union Canal along with the railway, industry began to settle in the town. Factories appeared close to the centre, making carpets and footwear, as did warehouses and a corn mill. Now the main roads are built up with turn-of-the-century and later red brick housing, the cinema on the Northampton Road has closed, and small supermarkets are springing up, just like any other town.

72276   ST NICHOLAS CHURCH, LITTLE BOWDEN, MARKET HARBOROUGH. Swallowed up by the suburbs of Market Harborough, the little village has managed to salvage some individuality. The small medieval church with its double bellcote form a centrepiece to a few houses of interest, including the Rectory of 1827 and the old Manor House of 1700.

72271   LEICESTER ROAD, MARKET HARBOROUGH. A rural tree-lined road where children can feel at ease and little danger threatens to befall the solitary cyclist. Now, cars leaving the town centre accelerate up and away towards Gallows Hill and The Kibworths.

72270   HIGH STREET, MARKET HARBOROUGH. A deserted street funnels into the town centre: Sunday morning perhaps? Beyond the high brick wall with its iron restraints, a very good array of Georgian houses lead the eye into the market place and on to St Dionysius Church.

72266   ST DIONYSIUS CHURCH AND OLD GRAMMAR SCHOOL, MARKET HARBOROUGH. The classic market town juxtaposition of church and grammar school create an ideal composition. The beautiful crocketted spire soars above the town, almost dwarfing the pretty timber faced school building. In the background, behind the school, is the Symingtons Corset Factory.

72262   HIGH STREET, MARKET HARBOROUGH. The High Street, earlier called the Great Street, is lined either side with Georgian buildings which sit at the head of earlier burgage plots, much the same as at Uxbridge, Middlesex or St Ives, Huntingdonshire. The wide street provided the place where townsfolk and country visitors could barter or sell goods on a day-to-day basis, and although more apparent from the air, it widens considerably either side of the church.

M33021   THE OLD GRAMMAR SCHOOL, MARKET HARBOROUGH. In the eighteenth century the almost picturesque group of church and school was completed by the addition of the town stocks and whipping post. The high quality timberwork in this essentially early seventeenth century building is visible in the open ground floor. The exterior of the upper storey consists of modern, planted boarding and pargeted plaster.

M33039   HIGH STREET, MARKET HARBOROUGH. Gone are the market stalls and booths of an earlier era. Here are the vans and accoutrements of a modern thriving market town, utilising the fronts of the Georgian buildings. The shops on the left of the photograph probably conceal timber frames of the seventeenth century or earlier.

M33094　　　HIGH STREET, MARKET HARBOROUGH. Just to the north of the church, the buildings on the west side of the road take on a varied appearance, the most special being the Three Swans Hotel, which has its origins from at least the early seventeenth century. Boots the Chemist offers just a glimpse of 60s design, while Woolworths appear to have changed little since the 1930s.

72265　　　THE MEMORIAL CROSS, MARKET HARBOROUGH. Market Harborough's tribute to the fallen, occupies pride of place in The Square, originally called the Sheep Market, which lies at the southern end of the market place. Behind the cross, Adam and Eve Street leads up to the former corsetry factory. Over the years encroachments have closed down this open space, but this may be excused by the quality of the flat - fronted Georgian buildings in the photograph.

M33107   Foxton Locks, Market Harborough. From the foot of the Foxton flight of locks, the canal cuts through the classic late eighteenth century enclosure landscape of straight hedges. The canal was built here in 1808-14, and a narrowboat trip through the ten locks would take about an hour. The cottage to the left of the photograph and the elegant brick bridge would appear to be contemporary with the date of the canal. Because of the length of time it took to go through the locks, an inclined plane was built between

1897-1900, which raised or lowered the narrowboats from one end to the other in under ten minutes. By about 1930 this amazing piece of engineering was in a state of disuse and the metal parts were sold as scrap. The extant remains have been classed as an Ancient Monument, but at the time of writing they are in a slowly decaying condition and included in the Register of Buildings At Risk published by English Heritage.

M33012   The Square, Market Harborough. A classic view of a market town. The open space around the square and the High Street to the north, bounded by well-mannered Georgian houses. Nineteenth century encroachments on the right of the photograph do not distract from the beauty of the church which dominates the photograph.

72272   CANAL BRIDGE, MARKET HARBOROUGH. Designed and constructed as a working tool, canals have become some of the most attractive and restful waterways in Britain. The rawness of the original cut has softened, and bridges have about them a mellowness so apparent in the photograph.

72273   THE WOODEN BRIDGE, MARKET HARBOROUGH. Just a plain wooden bridge, but it was a bridge such as this, upon which Edward Thomas stood in 1915, when for a few moments he imagined himself to linger between the past and the future or between life and death. Feelings which he was later to translate so beautifully into his poem - *The Bridge*.

72274   CANAL BOAT HOUSES, MARKET HARBOROUGH. The canal with its towing path, a symbol of an industrial age, has taken on a mantle of leisure. The bridge, contemporary with the cutting of the waterway, provides an ideal backdrop to the little armada of pleasure craft.

M33105   FOXTON LOCKS, MARKET HARBOROUGH. From the wide basin at the foot of the locks the prospect of climbing the flight by narrow boat is daunting. The area incorporating once this purely industrial facility, has now become a popular choice as an afternoon excursion into the country to escape from the city.

MELTON MOWBRAY

Melton Mowbray, a Domesday village, some fifteen miles north-east of Leicester, takes the second part of its name from the Norman lord, Roger de Mowbray, of about 1125. This quite small town has three remarkable claims to fame. Firstly, it can safely be called the fox hunting capital of the Shires, where up to the Second World War, royalty could come unmolested, to ride during the day and flirt during the night. Secondly, the town is the home of the world famous pork pie, which was probably invented to feed hungry huntsmen as early as the fourteenth century. The recipe has changed over the years, the original containing currants, raisins and anchovies, as well as pork. The town's third claim to fame is its association with Stilton cheese, which originated at Quenby Hall, to the south of the town, and was first called Quenby Cheese. The real cheese is made at Melton and its surrounding villages. Park the car, visit the church and purchase two gastronomic delights before moving on.

80309   ST MARY'S CHURCH, CHURCH STREET, MELTON MOWBRAY. This is probably the most beautiful of all Leicestershire churches, floating here above the trees and grassland, its magnificent late fifteenth century tower dominating the market place and the south side of the town. The fine porch once provided cover for the town fire engine.

80313   St Mary's Church, (North Transept), Melton Mowbray. Paid for by the priory of Lewes in Sussex in about 1300, the architecture represents a triumph of the stone mason's art, so much so that the church was championed as a possible contender for the new cathedral in 1926. The elaborate brass chandelier dates from 1746.

85169   MARKET PLACE, MELTON MOWBRAY. Crowds gather under tented canopies and round trestle-tabled market stalls, to snatch up bargains, just as they have done for 500 years. Good eighteenth century buildings dominate the scene. Note the former Swan Inn of the late seventeenth century on the extreme right of the photograph.

M60079   BURTON STREET, MELTON MOWBRAY. Burton Street refers to the former leper hospital of St Mary and St Lazars established about 1150 by Robert de Mowbray, to the south of the town, and seen now only as a series of earthworks to the north of Burton Lazars Hall.

M60094   TOWN CENTRE, MELTON MOWBRAY. Older buildings are to be found behind the innocuous façades of eighteenth and nineteenth century prosperity in Melton, which was boosted by it being at the centre of the hunting world, and by its prosperous cattle market.

M60031   NOTTINGHAM STREET, MELTON MOWBRAY. The early nineteenth century Bell Hotel dominates this lively street scene, with its vital interaction of stalls, traffic and people, now so often lost in the bromide world of pedestrianisation. Further along the street the former Italianate Corn Exchange with its rather odd timer bell tower can be seen.

M60097   SOUTH PARADE, MELTON MOWBRAY. In this predominately nineteenth century street, it is the once familiar that takes the eye. The delivery boy with his white coat and bicycle basket, and the unattended pram outside Mason's shop: in today's world it is no longer even a possibility for the modern mother.

M60072   SHERRARD STREET, MELTON MOWBRAY. Although the bicycle is making a comeback in the 1990s, the sight of so many propped against the kerb and quite happily left, is past. A large chain and stout lock are today's essentials or, better still, remove the front wheel before leaving.

M60011 ANNE OF CLEAVES HOUSE, BURTON STREET, MELTON MOWBRAY. One of the finest houses in the town and dating from the fifteenth century, it is likely to have been built as a priest's lodging. The name is linked to the church's connection with Lewes Priory and its revenues, which became the Queen's jointure.

M60027 THE CATTLE MARKET, MELTON MOWBRAY. The clothes of the traders may have changed, but Melton has been at the centre of the sheep farming industry for a number of centuries. From a time in the fifteenth century when the people of villages such as Ingarsby were ejected, and the more profitable sheep were moved in by the monks of Leicester Abbey.

M60028   THE CATTLE MARKET, MELTON MOWBRAY. The sheep, destined to become English mutton, may look bored, but to these men they are living money. Any fluctuation in prices can mean the difference between considerable wealth or months of hard work all for nothing.

M60068   LADY WILTON'S BRIDGE, PLAY CLOSE, MELTON MOWBRAY. The elegant, five-arched ashlar bridge of around 1830 is named after the Countess of Wilton, who's husband - a well-know figure in the hunting world, bought Egerton Lodge and entertained the rich and famous until he died in 1882.

M60012   ST EGELWIN THE MARTYR, SCALFORD, MELTON MOWBRAY. To the north of Melton Mowbray a good church of ironstone and limestone dating from the late twelfth century, with a south aisle of *c.*1270. The tower was rebuilt around 1640 and the rather solid looking chancel was added in 1845. There are no notable fitments or fittings in the church.

M60056   THE BELVOIR HUNT, MELTON MOWBRAY. Whether it is something to love or to hate, the hunt, with all its colourful trappings has proved to be much needed employment in the Shires since the eighteenth century. Tradition, spectacle and danger are here, bound tightly to the timeless bond between man and horse, and man and dog.

MOUNTSORREL

It is said that Mountsorrel had more pubs for its size than anywhere else in the country, presumably to cater for the influx of quarry workers. Since the eighteenth century the town has been the birthplace of numberless pink granite setts and kerb-stones originally for the turnpike, but some spread by waterway, countrywide. Working the hard stone produced great amounts of waste which eventually took over quarry production, producing granite chippings, particularly useful for railway ballast.

Granted market status in 1292, the town was more famous for its fair. The domed rotunda stands in the market place and was built in 1793, but even this addition does little to enliven the area. It is difficult to enthuse about either of the town's two churches, St Peter's, basically medieval and built in local granite, and Christ Church built around 1845 and of little interest. A town for the industrial archaeologist, where granite and slate blend together by the former wharves of the canal.

M2363270   MARKET PLACE, MOUNTSORREL. Remnants of the Earl of Leicester's castle which was destroyed in the early thirteenth century can still be seen in this rather dismal village. The plain red brick house is, however, a veritable gem, built around 1780 and prominent towards the left of the photograph.

M2363269   THE GREEN MOUNTSORREL. Hardly picturesque, crouched under the outcrop of granite, is a collection of small cottages, the earlier one probably occupied by the granite workers who came from as far away as Scotland to quarry and work the hard stone.

M2363268   THE RIVER SOAR, MOUNTSORREL. To the east of the village, the canalised river was heavily used for carrying stone, and waggon tipplers for loading up the boats can still be seen. The pleasure craft in the photograph emphasise the failure of the canals for industrial transportation.

OAKHAM

Oakham is the county town of Rutland, a proud name which has recently been right restored after the 1970s fiasco, when it was obliterated by merging it into Leicestershire. The town has remained small, notwithstanding some twentieth century expansion particularly on its western fringes, and since the creation of Rutland Water, it has become an ideal centre from which to sample its aquatic pleasures. For the walker, excursions to the beautiful Elizabethan church at Brook, or to the great house and church at Burley-on-the Hill, should not prove arduous. In the town centre there are few disruptive elements, the golden stone of the buildings enhancing views along the High Street, and in particular the area around the market place. The surviving hall within the castle earthworks served as a local court room until 1970, with its famous collection of horseshoes occupying much of the wall space, each donated by peers of the realm on their first visits to the town. The interest of Oakham is generally concentrated into a comparatively small area, but visitors should allow time to wander.

80295 THE CASTLE AND ALL SAINTS CHURCH, OAKHAM. A beautiful group. The fourteenth century tower and spire of the parish church dominates the market place and school to its south, while to the east, the castle remains combine to produce the classic juxtaposition of lordly and ecclesiastical dominance.

80290   ALL SAINTS CHURCH (NAVE AND CHANCEL), OAKHAM. The church is an elegant creation of around 1300, with a tall, slim five-bay arcade and clerestorey, creating a tremendous feeling of space. The arcade capitals are carved with biblical scenes, mixed up with birds and animals. The flower-decked font is dated around 1225.

85153   THE HAWTHORNE HORSE, OAKHAM. Photographed in 1932, this horse represents a supremely ironic comment. Here is the hunter, bred to cross in safety the open pastures of the Shires, formed in the enclosures' favourite hedge planting material, which makes up the obstacles to its safe progress.

Q12003 THE VILLAGE STREET, QUENIBOROUGH. Queniborough has the good fortune to be sited away from major roads, although it has become almost lined to industrial Syston. The main street is wide with a fine collection of houses of various dates, styles and materials. In the photograph only the telegraph pole and its wires intrude into the scene.

Q12001 THE VILLAGE AND ST MARY'S CHURCH, QUENIBOROUGH. Virtually a part of the outer edge of suburban Leicester, the photograph presents an almost chocolate box view of the village. The thatched cruck cottage, with its museum piece petrol pump and the amazing interlocking of roofs, lead the eye inexorably to the needle-like spire, which crowns the pink granite tower of the church. Internally, the building lacks any quality monuments, apart from a brass plate commemorating Margaret Bury who died in 1633. In the early 1980s, vestry and complimentary rooms were built into the west end of the church.

QUORN

The mention of Quorn immediately brings to mind one of the premier English hunts, probably only to be equalled in fame by the Belvoir, but it is a pity the village fails to reflect the colourful splendour associated with its namesake. Its medieval church of Norman foundation houses good monuments, in particular one of 1587 to Sir John Farnham, by Epiphanius Evesham, whose fine cutting and virtuosity in design raises him above almost every other English sculptor of the sixteenth century. Many of the village houses are built of local granite and Swithland slate, and Bridge Mills pays tribute to the village as a place of manufacturing.

Q11018   HIGH STREET, QUORN. The village sits astride the A6, only two miles north of Mountsorrel, and although deeply embedded in granite country, the buildings in the photograph, lack any of that hard-edged quality. Red brick workers cottages face timber and render on the opposite side of the road, speaking of softer parts of the country.

Q11020   THE HURST HOTEL, QUORN. Photographed in 1965, a classic Edwardian hotel, with its tile hung gables, bracketed enclosed balcony and original fenestration. On the right, a contemporary wing of singular quality lurks behind the petrol pumps. For show, transportation of an earlier age adorns the forecourt.

Q11004   THE RIVER SOAR, QUORN. A swan cruises on the river as it curves into the east side of the village, running by a municipalised garden of finely mown grass, and a statutory wooden seat carefully placed under the only tree of consequence.

ROTHLEY

Rothley lies some five miles to the north of Leicester and to the west of the busy A6. Although the village is close to the River Soar, it was not until the arrival of the railway that it began to expand. An early housing estate was laid out around 1910 by Parker and Unwin, who were much involved in the design of the famous pioneering development of Hampstead Garden Suburb, London. Thomas Babington Macaulay, Rothley's most famous son, was born at Rothley Temple on St Crispin's Day, 1800, the son of the anti-slaver, Zachary Macaulay. Thomas became Whig M.P.for Calne, Leeds, but it was his masterpiece - "History of England", that brought him undying fame. In historic building terms the temple is one of the important houses in the county, and as Rothley Court Hotel, it is readily accessible. The village is rich in vernacular houses, and the visitor will not be unrewarded.

R259010   ST MARY AND ST JOHN THE BAPTIST CHURCH, ROTHLEY. The large size of this Charnwood commuter village is hardly reflected in such an idyllic scene as this, a curving roadway with modest houses leading directly to the west door of the thirteenth century church, housing a good series of monuments. In the churchyard is a cross shaft dating, it is said, to the ninth century.

R259002   WOODGATE, ROTHLEY. The mundane surburban face of the village, which has grown around a core of rather special later medieval houses and the Rothley Temple, built on Knights Templar land around.1315. Along with Temple Church, London and Temple Balsall, Warwickshire, the chapel is one of the finest in England.

R259001   MILKING TIME, ROTHLEY. A scene which is familiar to us all, even in the rush of today's "rat-run" world. Plodding cows head for the milking parlour, guided by the farmer on his wobbly upright bicycle.

SOUTH WIGSTON

As late as 1870, enclosure meadowland and hawthorn hedges stretched away from Wigston Magna, but the ensuing period up to 1900 was to see a trebling in population figures, and the appearance of hosiers and boot and shoe manufacturers from Leicester, looking for potential factory sites. By 1885, thanks to the endeavours of Orson Wright a speculative developer, the grid pattern of streets and terraces had begun to be laid down, to house the influx of workers. Engine sheds bounded the railway along with the new brick and tile works. Many people arrived to take up employment in this small booming new town, and in 1894 it became an Urban district, in a period of rolling industrialisation. Epitomising working life, a Mechanics Institute, a National School, and a Working Mens Club were built, for what amounted to a new style of society. Finally, public utilities were installed to complete what we now perceive as a depressing Victorian picture.

S487003   LEICESTER ROAD, SOUTH WIGSTON. The only reason to want to visit South Wigston is that either you live there or you have friends that live there. Built alongside the Leicester-Rugby railway line, its main unhappy attribute is to be found in a variety of factories and works producing anything from biscuits to shoes.

S548023   BLABY ROAD, SOUTH WIGSTON. It was W.G. Hoskins, who said of South Wigston that "it reaches the rock bottom of English provincial life," and it would be hard to disagree with his sentiments. The railway, factories and the brick terraces are to be avoided unless travelling from the M1 to Oadby, or to the racecourse.

S487016   THE MEMORIAL, SOUTH WIGSTON. A rather choleric lion sits on top of a strangely classical, island memorial cum clock tower. The total street scene exudes 1900, with rather uninviting shops and an unalluring corner pub. Even the boys hanging about seem to compliment the overall ambience of the area.

S548008   CROW MILL, SOUTH WIGSTON. Crow Mill which was recorded on the River Sence around the mid-twelfth century, is seen here in a picturesque meadowland setting. Close to the canal it was bought by the canal's owners, and with the installation of a steam engine it worked until around 1900.

TWYCROSS

Twycross is not surrounded by villages of outstanding interest, but to its east is Gopsall Park, on the site of Gopsall, the deserted medieval village. The house, built by Charles Jennens in 1747, and designed by John Westley, a local architect in a loosely Palladian manner, was the grandest house in West Leicestershire.

In what amounts to an appalling act of vandalism the house was demolished in 1951. The village is not well equipped with vernacular houses of special quality, but the Old Hall near the church must be noted.

Although mainly of the early fourteenth century, the architecture of the church takes a very definite second place to the magnificent medieval east window. Said to have come from the Saint-Chapelle in Paris and presented to King William IV, it is a breath-taking example of the thirteenth century French, stained-glass artists work. Many visitors come to Twycross for the zoo, but stop off in the village to see a superb work of art.

T237006   THE VILLAGE STREET, TWYCROSS. Its position on the A444 between Nuneaton and Burton-on-Trent is belied in this rural ideal. The cows, with their drover, the cottages ranged behind small gardens and picket fences, and the church tower in the background, add up to a satisfactory whole, of which William Morris would have approved.

UPPINGHAM

As attractive as almost any Midland market town, Uppingham is surrounded by stone villages of outstanding quality. To the south, Lyddington with its wide main street and Bede House, originally a part of the Bishop of Lincoln's Palace, now in the care of English Heritage, and a mile or so to its west, Stoke Dry, a single street on a steep hill running down to Eye Brook Resevoir. Here is a church, where the Gunpowder plotters are said to have met and lingered in, with its strange carving, wall paintings, and Digby monuments. To the north of the town, and almost in a line from east to west are the stone villages of Wing, with its maze Preston and Ridlington.

When W.G.Hoskins wrote his *Shell Guide to Rutland* in 1963, he noted specially that motoring in the county was still a pleasure. To a great extent those days it must be said have gone, but even now, once away from the main roads, backwaters such as atmospheric Stockerston, Brooke or Tixover can be enjoyed in peace. The area will provide a relaxing, unhurried weekend. Park the car, walk or cycle and just soak up the landscape.

85156   THE MARKET PLACE, UPPINGHAM. Little seems to have altered in the market place since the eighteenth century. The square seems quite small now for a town which has had an extremely active market since the thirteenth century. The grand church of St Peter and St Paul, which oversees the goings-on, is from the fourteenth century, but it was badly mauled in a restoration of 1842.

U10013   HIGH STREET, UPPINGHAM. Uppingham is a particularly attractive town with an attractive series of seventeenth and eighteenth century buildings. Surprisingly, the shop fronts in the photograph, have, in the main, been preserved, presumably at the behest of a vigilant local council. The street bustles today in the best possible way.

80317   UPPINGHAM SCHOOL, HIGH STREET, UPPINGHAM. During the medieval period, grammar schools were founded for the education of scholars across the class spectrum, but by the eighteenth century, the so-called Great Schools had arrived in England. Founded in 1584 by Archdeacon Johnson in a single-roomed building, the Uppingham School complex expanded vastly during the last century.

85164   UPPINGHAM SCHOOL, HIGH STREET, UPPINGHAM. Whereas Harrow School occupies buildings spread out along the main village streets, Uppingham takes on the qualities of a university, being, in the main, laid out around quadrangles. The buildings range in date from the end of the sixteenth century to those of Drew-Edwards Keen, of the 1980s.

72280   THE VICTORIA TOWER, HIGH STREET, UPPINGHAM. The tower has provided a daunting welcome to generations of potential pupils. Although appearing to be medieval, it was designed by Sir Thomas Jackson in 1815. In the recess, is a statue of the school's founder, by Sir George Frampton.

85159   ST PETER AND ST PAUL'S CHURCH AND SCHOOL, UPPINGHAM. This panoramic view of the church and school from flower-bedecked meadow land, sum up the qualities of this self contained town. In 1932, England was not familiar with today's chemically controlled, monocrop pastures, nor was it a challenge to buy home grown fruit in the shops.

80323   SCHOOL QUADRANGLE, UPPING-HAM. The air of a monastic undercroft pervades the photograph with its heavy circular columns and chamfered pointed arches. Architectural greats such as G.E. Street, Ernest Newton and later, Oliver Hill worked on the school buildings, a classic collection of their kind.

WIGSTON MAGNA

Four miles south of Leicester, medieval Wigstone was a large nucleated village, standing in the middle of its three great fields. With the 1766 Enclosure award came a replanned landscape of small fields overlying the former ridge and furrow furlongs, and industrialisation, which increased its population, brought with it fever and consumption to raise the death rate. Leicester's well organised hosiery manufacturers hired out their knitting frames to smaller village masters, who, in turn, rented them to their operatives. The first railway station opened in 1839 and a second in 1857, with at one time, some 300 railway workers living in Station Road. Victorian buildings began to blot out the earlier village street pattern, with the appearance of red brick workers cottages, a National School, and a Mechanics Institute. A Framework Knitting Museum is open to the public in Bushloe End. Of Wigston's churches, All Saints, dates from around 1300, but St Wistans, although superficially medieval, was built in 1853. W.G Hoskins book, *The Midland Peasant,* written in 1957 paints a wonderful word picture of the village from its origins to 1900.

W366052   THE MEMORIAL PARK, WIGSTON MAGNA. In the angle between Long Street and Chapel Lane, is this absolutely classic example of a municipal memorial park. The serpentine edging, designer boulders and statutory pavilion are to be seen in almost every suburb of Leicester in varied forms.

WOODHOUSE EAVES

Woodhouse Eaves, situated in the heart of the ancient forest of Charnwood, first appears as Wodehuses, literally meaning the houses in the woods, around 1210. With its close neighbour, Swithland, it is associated with a vast output of slate during the eighteenth and nineteenth centuries, for use as a roofing material and for graveyard headstones. Its ability to take the most intricate of carving and to weather well, put it among the most popular of materials, to such an extent that almost every churchyard in the county can show examples, often these days, used as paving. During the nineteenth century an influx of Welsh slate overwhelmed the local quarries. In Swithland Wood, to the south of the village, the disused slate workings can be seen amongst the bluebells, for which the area was well known. Overlooking the village, Windmill Hill was crowned by one of the county's post mills until it was destroyed by fire in 1945.

W367010   THE VILLAGE, WOODHOUSE EAVES. St Pauls Church of 1837, by William Railton, dominates the village with its intricate pattern of roofs. Railton exhibited at the Royal Academy, and was architect to the Church Commissioners from 1838-48. Apart from working in Leicestershire, he designed Nelson's Column in Trafalgar Square and was also employed on Ripon Minster, Yorkshire.

W367041 WOODHOUSE EAVES FROM THE MEMORIAL. In walking country, the village, although undistinguished, is associated by local people with Newton Linford, Bradgate Park and Beacon Hill, or just as being on the back route from Leicester to Shepshed. The garage on the extreme right of the photograph emphasises the easy pace of 1950s motoring.

W367053 MAIN STREET, WOODHOUSE EAVES. Quarrymen's cottages, and the archetypal Pear Tree pub, give no hint of the attractions of the surrounding countryside. Bradgate Park, only a stones throw away, where Lady Jane Grey, the ill-fated nine day queen, lived in the now ruined house, is a favourite beauty spot away from the city.

W367024   CHARNWOOD FOREST
CONVALESCENT HOME. To be ill as a child
after the war, was considered worthwhile if
it meant spending time away by being sent
to the home to recuperate. It was, however,
always just as good to return home again.

W367089   VIEW FROM OLD JOHN,
WOODHOUSE EAVES. Crowning the highest
point in Bradgate Park, the views from this
eighteenth century prospect tower are
among the finest in the county. Although
given to and administered by the City Council
since 1928, the much-visited park, enclosed
around 1250, has not lost any of its essential
rugged character.

Pictorial Memories Collection

A great new range of publications featuring the work of innovative Victorian photographer Francis Frith.

∞ 1998 Titles ∞

County Series £9.99

1-84125-045-7	Berkshire	
053-8	Buckinghamshire	
024-4	Derbyshire	
077-5	Greater London	
028-7	Kent	
029-5	Lake District	
051-1	Lancashire	
031-7	Leicestershire	
026-0	London	
027-9	Norfolk	
030-9	Sussex	
063-5	West Yorkshire	
025-2	Yorkshire	

Town & City Series £9.99

010-4	Brighton & Hove	
015-5	Canterbury	
079-1	Edinburgh	
012-0	Glasgow & Clydeside	
081-3	Norwich	
040-6	York	

Country Series £9.99

1-84125-075-9	Ireland	
071-6	North Wales	
073-2	Scotland	
069-4	South Wales	

Poster Books £4.99

000-7	Canals and Waterways	
032-5	Derbyshire	
001-5	High Days and Holidays	
036-8	Kent	
037-6	Lake District	
034-1	London	
005-8	Railways	

£5.99

023-6	Canterbury	
043-0	Derby	

∞ Titles from January to July 1999 ∞

County Series £9.99

1-84125-049-x	Warwickshire	March
047-3	Staffordshire	
057-0	Devon	
067-8	Cheshire	
065-1	Nottinghamshire	
059-7	Cornwall	

1-84125-101-1	Surrey	
095-3	Hampshire	
128-3	Highlands	April
149-6	Hertfordshire	
130-5	North Yorkshire	May
150-x	Wiltshire	

Town & City Series £7.99

089-9	Maidstone	March
087-2	Bradford	
083-x	Colchester	
093-7	Dublin	
091-0	Leeds	
105-4	Buxton	
111-9	Bristol	
113-5	Nottingham	
011-2	Manchester	
107-0	Matlock	
009-0	Macclesfield	April
132-1	St Ives	
008-2	Derby	
113-x	Sevenoaks	
014-7	Newbury	
134-8	Bognor Regis	
144-5	Leicester	
145-3	East Grinstead	
146-1	Newark	

137-2	Sheffield	May
138-0	Cambridge	
139-9	Penzance	
140-2	Eastbourne	
147-x	Llandudno	
142-9	Torquay	
148-8	Whitby	
159-3	Scarborough	June
160-7	Faversham to Herne Bay	
164-x	Scilly Isles	
162-3	Dorset Coast	
168-2	Falmouth	
165-8	Newquay	
154-2	Bakewell	July
163-1	Lincoln	
167-4	Barnstaple	
174-7	Great Yarmouth	
141-0	Blackpool	
207-7	Dartmoor	

WATERTON PRESS, WATERTON ESTATE, BRIDGEND, GLAMORGAN, CF31 3XP.
TEL: 01656 668836   FAX: 01656 668710

Voucher

This voucher entitles you to a half price mounted print normally *£19.95*

*Mounted prints are A4 sepia, mounted in a cream mount with beval cut aperture and single burgundy ruled line, greyboard backing and cello bagged.

Special offer price £9.97

Simply select the view in this book that you would like to receive as a mounted print, and complete the form below.

Page & Negative Number	Town & Description

I enclose a cheque/postal order for £9.97 which includes p&p, made payable to "The Francis Frith Collection."

Name & Address:

Mr/Mrs/Miss/Ms

Initial   Surname

Address

Town

County

Postcode

Daytime Telephone No.
(incase of queries)

Send your voucher and remittance to:
The Francis Frith Collection
Dept FF006, 'Friths Barn', Teffont,
Salisbury, Wilts, SP3 5QP.